Adventures On the Wild Side

A poetry and photo introspective on connecting with the beauty and wonder of the natural world.

ISBN: 978-1-989872-19-2

First Published in Canada, 2026.
Published by Southernwood Technologies Inc. 2026.

Visit **cheryllawson.net/cherylbezphotobooks** for more information.

Also by Cheryl Bez:
The Romance of Flowers (ISBN: 978-1-989872-15-4)

For Mum

We'll meet again at the beach

CONTENTS

Mountains Majestic

In the silence of the snow,

the alpine ridge rears up,

pushing me towards the sky.

The unending stillness proclaims its power

with what is left unsaid.

This solitude is prized,

yearned for, in an overcrowded world.

Up here, the great stillness is company enough.

Rivers birthed in snowmelt tumble and cascade
over uneven earth that gives up the easiest path.
Water ribbons across mountaintops, coursing down, down,
down.

The drip turned trickle.
The stream turned torrent.
The plunge giving way to lazy meander.

How magnificent the waterfall in its season!
Thunderous energy, life carried coastward.
Spray lingers, the dew a saturated coolness.

Plunge pools roil,
the keepers of mysterious depths.
Tree and fern cling, siphoning life from green rocks.
An existence perilous, yet glorious,
caught in the rush, yet timeless.

Peaks and Valleys,
Cliffs and Crests.
Glaciers and Meadows.

Mere words.

Tiny and insufficient monikers
for indescribable beauty.
Useless tags for what lies out there.
That which our imaginations cannot fathom
without a sighting,
without reference of scale:

The awe of
the horizon-capturing,
view-dominating spectacle
of earth rising heavenward.

Wake Up!

A mundane life is only a slow death.
The sleepwalker will never know the pain and pleasure
of bracing cold, of perilous climbs on tired legs.
Instead a fog settles, a ghostly iniquity,
leaching triumph and agony;
numbness a fake reward.
Screen taps steal life, victories, memories.
Byte-sized moments thrill less and less.
The mad machine men hold the world hostage.

Wake Up!
Break Out!
LIVE!
For more than just today.
Frosted air, dirt underfoot.
Build the bridge to an aware self.
Heed the wilderness calling,
A promise of vivid horizons and pastoral flowers.
Riches await, the wild awake and waiting.

Woodland
Wander

The leaf,
The wing,
The furry little thing.
The moss,
The log,
The swampy, damp bog.
The frost,
The snow,
The hibernation burrow.
The new,
The old,
The budding and the mold.
The short,
The tall,
A season for them all.

Make room for the wild things.
For in doing so,
imagination finds a home.

Push the drift.

Fight for footing on powdered ground.

Familiar landmarks a fleeting gift.

Snow-laden trees.

Huddle low, the cold profound.

The white stuff blown on frigid breeze.

Clearings made blue-white.

Fresh snow squeak and scrunch,

Winter's own sound.

Drifting flakes shimmer cold and bright.

The Path Finder

One who is brave, capable and prepared for adventure

To trod the path with eager feet,
To leave the city, the lights and streets.
To feel the sun, and hear the wind,
To know Nature's peace deep within.

Shake off the madness, ease the crush,
Absorb and sense the forest's hush.
The heart expands, the mind at rest,
Restored; uplifted by Nature's best.

Autumn wind lifts leaves aloft,
It's voice a mournful groan.
The fledgling season's over,
the young, at last, have flown.
There, a birdhouse hangs:
Quiet. Lonely. Still.
The chicks have gone.
The brood is done.
No more hungry mouths to fill.
For those who flew: no regret, no pangs.
The quiet wood is home.
Huddled for warmth in bramble, on branch,
The flock sings bright and sweet.
Their puffed-up will to survive the chill
Matched perfectly to Nature's beat.

Life's a Beach

Ocean Indigo, deep and dark, hides secret lives,
Anemones, sea stars, squid and plankton,
A world separate and alien thrives.

Yet humans feel it's ours to conquer,
As if we own it all.
Disregard the plights, ignore the danger,
Control and riches – a siren call.

Greatest world on Earth
we cry, outraged.
Preservation and protection:
can we get them to engage?
No.
Their greed has cut our ties to her,
the result could be destruction.

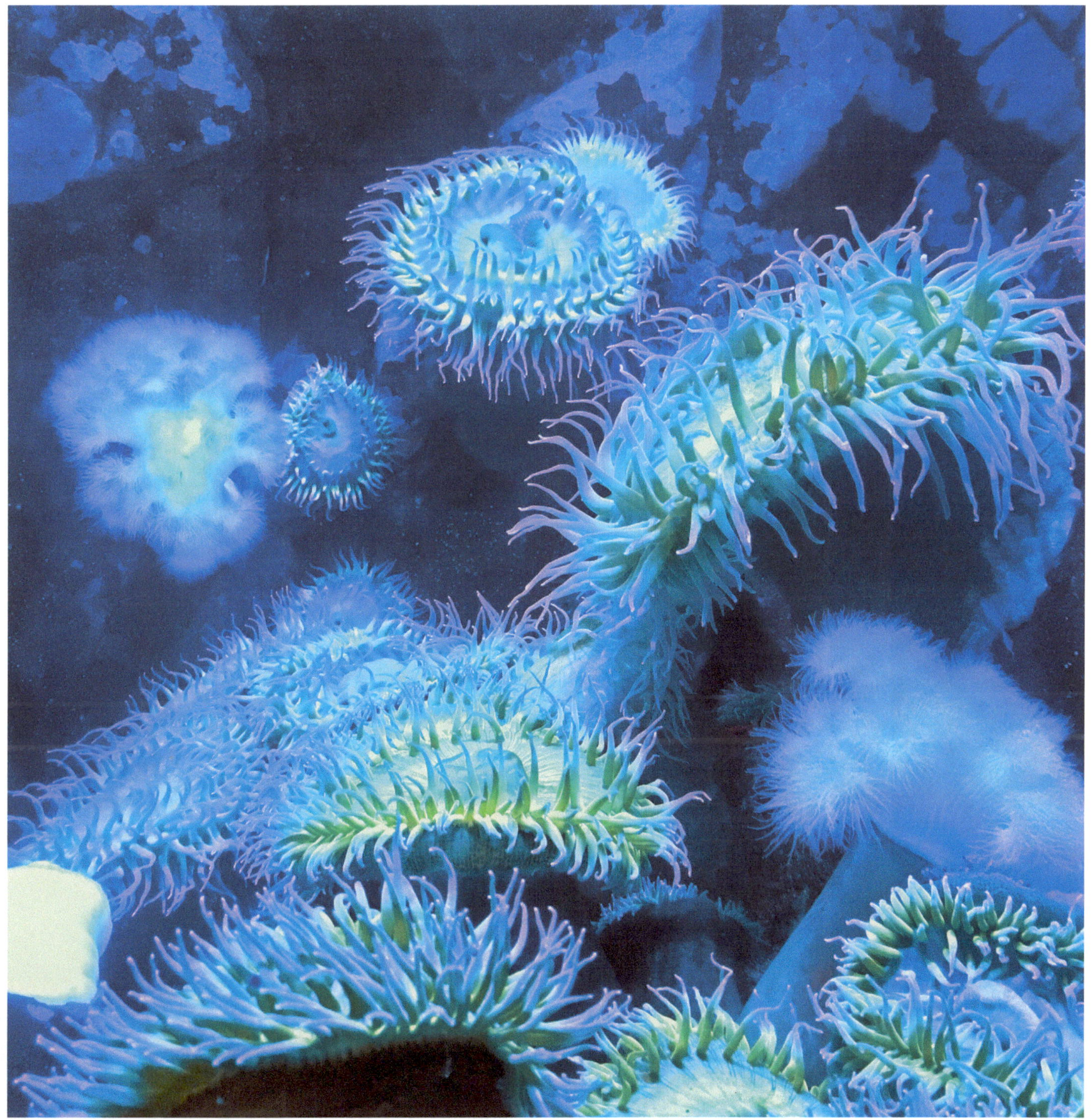

Birds of a Feather

are stronger together

Flocked and feathered,
Huddled and hungry.
The next meal coming soon.
Wings expanded,
drying and sunning,
Cormorants on piers commune.
Webbed feet on mud,
wait out the tide, shells hint at treasure stored.
A gull's delight, shared not with mates,
Juicy leftovers he has scored.
"We're here for more," the Eagles say,
eyes trained on bigger fish.
The gleam of scale, and flick of fin,
salmon pink their dinner dish.

Nothing heals quite so well

the painful edges of life

as

The Blue Horizon

Dock & Pier

The promise of Sea.
Boardwalk and brine,
Saltwater sweetness
for the Soul.

The Art of
Getting Lost

Fen and fog, a world concealed.
Conspiring cloud hangs low.
Edges softened,
morphed and muted,
Shared secrets as we go.
Words spoken here in quiet tone,
For no one else's ears.
Winter's chill on frosted fences,
Drip watercolour tears.

Glass-smooth lake,
Rough-and-tumble river,
Kayak and canoe
wander waterways.
Paddlers seeking serenity,
Living the clear, blue moment,
Finding their Joy in the
bubbling,
lapping,
reflecting
wild water.

Fractal fantasy,
rock rings and leaf swirls.
The patterns organic,
Yet mesmerizing in their order.
Smooth-tumbled pebbles,
Weathered wood whirls.
Bark's growing symmetry,
Shapes, lines, folds visible,
A tale of Earth's artistry.

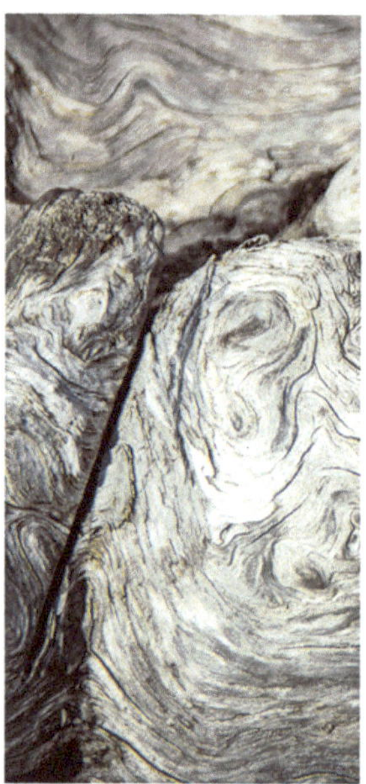

Look closer & discover

untold wealth

in the textures and patterns

of the natural world.

From driftwood to clouds,

Leaf to feather.

Life thrives in patterns.

Staggering contrast,

Surprising opposites,

Tiny to tall,

Found widely or discovered in one spot.

Extraordinary that nature nurtures such variety,

Spun from mundane to spectacular,

Life in every detail.

Thriving on change, growth and destruction.

Old to new, to old again.

Intersections

With Nature

Purposefully strolling the flower-edged paths.
Mindfully letting toes sink in at the shoreline.
Breathing in the salty air or forest tang or floral scent.
Touching light, tracing veins, feeling free.

Finding our way to the outdoors,
by whichever means gets us there,
restores meaning, depth, and life.
Restores a connection that makes us real,
makes us feel part of something profoundly amazing.

The tall, strong trees grow taller still,
and Nature presses in.
The tended path, well kept, holds court,
the boughs and grasses, loyal.

This magic is of earth and sky.
A world inside a world,
The secrets here, as old as time,
And too precious to be shared.

Where we walk the path, the magic follows.
The trees lay down Fall cloth,
and hail Time, the real king,
as each season comes and goes.

The purpose of life

might be

to tend the garden of your heart

so that those who know you are surrounded

by joy blooming from your soul,

by light beaming through your boughs,

and by abundant love

– the gift of yourself to others.

Choose winter snow or beach huts,
coursing turquoise rapids or muddy ruts.
Tiptoe past gurgling streams,
Cast wide your Mountain dreams,
Find Life's playful seams.
Hike and climb,
ski a hill.
Sway and slide,
Let loose the thrill.
Life is joy on all the faces,
in all the ways,
at all the places.
It's Great Outdoors time.
Grab your gear and do up your laces.

At the sea
we find ourselves
reflecting on our smallness,
as we gaze at the water's expanse.
We face our limits,
as the horizon meets the sky.
We understand that
even when we push in,
bring our humaness to the sea,
we are only holding back today's tides.
Our artificial world will fade,
The paint will dull,
The boardwalks will crumble; decay.
The sea is forever – its ebb and flow,
full of all the yesterdays, todays and tomorrows.

FIRE
LANE

Wonder is all around

waiting in plain sight.
In a still pool,
or on a quiet beach.
In a reflecting pond,
or a turquoise lake.
The pattern of feathers
or creak of branches.
The rhythm of waves,
the tumble of water.

Gems in nature
award riches beyond measure.
For every path walked
holds potential to discover.

This book is ended.
And we must go.
Let's meet at the river,
Or on the snow.

May the weather be fair
and the wind mild.
May the air be sweet,
and the nature, Wild.

Photography: Cheryl Bezuidenhout

Poetry and Prose: Cheryl Bezuidenhout

This book is dedicated to wanderers, both young and old. It is for those who seek peace in nature, who wish to preserve its beauty, and honour its importance in our lives.

Like my other photography-poetry book (**The Romance of Flowers**) this book, **Adventures On the Wild Side,** is presented as journeys to captivate and provoke thought and mindfulness, reverence and love, care and stewardship. I do hope you've enjoyed the poetry and pictures.

Thank you for reading.

www.ingramcontent.com/pod-product-compliance
Lightning Source LLC
LaVergne TN
LVHW070142110826
845147LV00002B/311

* 9 7 8 1 9 8 9 8 7 2 1 9 2 *